# Successful
# Leadership

Carol A. O'Connor, Ph.D.

*All inquiries should be addressed to:*
Barron's Educational Series, Inc.
250 Wireless Boulevard
Hauppauge, New York  11788

Library of Congress Catalog Card No. 96-17933

International Standard Book No. 0-7641-0072-6

**Library of Congress Cataloging-in-Publication Data**
O'Connor, Carol A., 1949–
    [Successful leadership in a week]
    Successful leadership / Carol A. O'Connor.
        p.    cm. — (Barron's business success series)
    Originally published: Successful leadership in a week.
London : Hodder & Stoughton, 1996.
    ISBN 0-7641-0072-6
    1. Leadership.    I. Title.    II. Series.
HD57.7.0358    1996
658.4'092—dc20                              96-17933
                                            CIP

PRINTED IN HONG KONG
9876543

# Contents

◆

**Introduction** . . . . . . . . . . . . . . . . . . . . . . . . . . . . . . . . . . . . . v

**Chapter 1**
Developing Awareness . . . . . . . . . . . . . . . . . . . . . . . . . . . . . . . 1

**Chapter 2**
Understanding People . . . . . . . . . . . . . . . . . . . . . . . . . . . . . 15

**Chapter 3**
Power and Authority . . . . . . . . . . . . . . . . . . . . . . . . . . . . . 27

**Chapter 4**
Communication . . . . . . . . . . . . . . . . . . . . . . . . . . . . . . . . . 41

**Chapter 5**
Decision Making . . . . . . . . . . . . . . . . . . . . . . . . . . . . . . . . 57

**Chapter 6**
Creating a Vision . . . . . . . . . . . . . . . . . . . . . . . . . . . . . . . . 75

**Chapter 7**
Taking Charge . . . . . . . . . . . . . . . . . . . . . . . . . . . . . . . . . . 87

**Index** . . . . . . . . . . . . . . . . . . . . . . . . . . . . . . . . . . . . . . . 94

# Introduction

◆

Everyone has leadership potential. Often it is modesty or a lack of confidence or experience that inhibits an individual from taking the lead. Even so, opportunities for leadership occur every day, so that even the most reluctant individuals occasionally find themselves in charge. The better prepared they are to meet leadership challenges, the more readily they develop new skills and increase in confidence and personal insight.

Leadership skill can be acquired through training and effort. This process often begins when individuals discover that they possess qualities and strengths usually associated with leadership. They surprise themselves with their inner resources. When this kind of inner strength is revealed, its existence is not easily forgotten. Regular exercise of newfound strength produces further achievement and a sense of self-fulfillment.

Each situation is different. Although important occasions are glamorous and attention-getting, more routine events benefit leadership development as well. Each chance to lead provides valuable practice, experience, and preparation for major events in the future.

Potential leaders also need to recognize that along with the role comes responsibility. Taking charge is never easy and effective leadership requires great effort. This means pressure, stress, and challenge, but also immense satisfaction when a task is successfully achieved.

Because most people are followers much of the time, part of every effort to develop leadership should include skills of following as well. The two sets of skills are complementary. A skilled supporter knows how to contribute to a leader's success, while a good leader acts on behalf of the supporters.

Seven areas are essential for successful leadership. Using a step-by-step approach, these basics will be explored in this book. The purpose is to improve your performance in both major and minor roles through better understanding of leadership requirements and through the practice of skills.

*Steps to successful leadership*

**1.** developing awareness

**2.** understanding people

**3.** power and authority

**4.** communication

**5.** decision making

**6.** creating a vision

**7.** taking charge

# Chapter 1

---

# Developing
# Awareness

The first step to successful leadership is development of self-aware-ness. Leaders need to take time to reflect on the strengths and weaknesses of their behavior. This provides a basis for improving performance as well as increasing confidence and understanding other people. Leaders who lack personal insight are like tone-deaf musicians. Even if they acquire technical accuracy through drill and practice, they begin each performance at a distinct disadvantage. They need a sense of art as well as science in order to recognize when they have hit a sour note.

This chapter covers four aspects of the development of self-awareness:

◆ leadership basics

◆ self-assessment

◆ following the leader

◆ personal development

## LEADERSHIP BASICS

There are three commonly accepted beliefs about leadership:

◆ Leaders are born to their role.

◆ Certain qualities make a leader, such as ambition, charisma, confidence, initiative, independence, creativity, and a sense of responsibility, among many others.

◆ Situations create leaders who emerge to meet the needs of a specific group, time, or place. When the task is finished, these leaders retire from their roles.

All three of these ideas appear in a variety of forms throughout history, and serious study of them has dominated military and business science in this century. Although the debate about the nature of leadership continues, each approach has its firm advocates. Even so, one issue is consistently relevant regardless of these beliefs. This is that leadership success depends upon the development of a positive relationship between leaders and supporters. The best leaders value their supporters and demonstrate this through their actions.

They know that respect is earned. It is the leaders' attitude towards their followers that inspires loyalty. This is far more important than birthright, personal qualities, a specific situation, or a combination of all of these. Supporters are important because without them, leadership exists only in the imagination of a would-be leader.

> *Leadership is the ability to present a vision so that others want to achieve it. It requires skill in building relationships with other people and organizing resources effectively. Mastery of leadership is open to everyone.*

The leader's tasks are to focus attention on a common purpose, to guide events, and to organize activity. Cooperation among colleagues is inspired by creating a shared sense of purpose and the awareness of the importance of the task. It requires self-confidence to encourage others to complete assigned tasks, and to monitor progress while always highlighting a common vision.

This confidence is drawn from a basic sense of respect that leaders have for themselves and other people. Ironically, those who already have self-respect receive recognition from others naturally. Those who need to develop this leadership essential have difficulty gaining the respect of others.

This process can begin in everyday life when potential leaders make an effort to understand the difficulties that challenge other people. When colleagues' problems are sincerely acknowledged, mutual appreciation tends to grow. This is the basis for giving and inevitably receiving respect.

There are leaders who gain power through bullying or manipulation. History and current news stories from politics and business show again and again that this behavior works in the short term only. Those leaders who inspire, build, create, and encourage their colleagues have long-term success and are remembered long into the future. Those who undermine, destroy, cheat, and belittle their followers are avoided as soon as their power begins to weaken—as it always does.

## SELF-ASSESSMENT

One source of information about leadership effectiveness is feedback from other people. It is certainly a valuable exercise to discover the impact of leadership behavior on colleagues. Occasionally, though, their remarks are biased, imprecise, or lack perception. How can a leader determine which comments are useful and which are not? This question is particularly challenging because it is so tempting to disregard negative comments or adopt a defensive attitude about them.

One answer to this problem is for leaders to assess their own performance first. This offers a baseline against which colleagues' comments, considered carefully, may be set. A strong self-image, clear goals for personal development, and high performance standards allow a leader to judge if comments are helpful, appropriate, or signal the need for a change in behavior.

Obviously, self-assessment requires the strictest honesty. It is a waste of time and opportunity to create a fantasy self-image. Also, this process needs discrimination so that an assessment of *current* leadership skills is distinguished from *future* performance goals. By recognizing the difference between "who I am now" and "who I want to be," leaders can produce a plan of action to achieve their goals for personal development.

## FOLLOWING THE LEADER

All sorts of questions come to mind when embarking on self-assessment:

◆ Am I fair?

◆ Do I take responsibility?

◆ Do I listen?

◆ Am I honest?

◆ Am I willing to debate?

◆ Do colleagues trust me?

The first challenge is to ask: "Do I lead in such a way that I would willingly follow myself?" Improved leadership performance is based on a careful study of *actual* behavior. It helps to think of a recent leadership experience and then focus on the details. Examining this specific performance allows an assessment of leadership skill for that occasion.

Begin the process by listing five positive and five negative features of *actual* and *current* leadership behavior.

### Positive leadership behavior

1

2

3

4

5

### Negative leadership behavior

1

2

**3**

**4**

**5**

This total of 10 features should readily come to mind. Fewer than 10 shows there is a strong need to develop better self-awareness; or, it could indicate a need for more leadership practice and experience. If either situation is the case, it is still of value to refer to the shorter list. At a later date, this activity should be repeated until the list includes at least 10 items.

The following is an example of how these lists might look.

### Positive leadership behavior

**1.** Shows fairness

**2.** Listens well

**3.** Exhibits integrity

**4.** Motivates team members

**5.** Knows project thoroughly

### Negative leadership behavior

**1.** Impatient with slow thinkers

**2.** Friendly with some team members, argumentative with others

**3.** Gives unclear directions

**4.** Does not share information/knowledge

**5.** Chooses friends for team, regardless of skills

The process of self-assessment can be continued by next considering colleagues' opinions and beliefs. Although this list depends upon guesswork, it is useful to attempt it. There is always a benefit to be gained by imagining a colleague's point of view and attempting to see the world from a different perspective. Again, draw up two lists, one containing five examples of colleagues' positive opinions and beliefs, one of five negative examples.

### Colleagues' positive beliefs

1

2

3

4

5

### Colleagues' negative beliefs

1

2

3

4

5

*Activity*

◆ Compare the two lists: personal and colleagues' perceptions.

◆ Are they the same throughout?

◆ If not, highlight the differences.

◆ If they are, ask yourself why; then repeat the exercise.

◆ How can you increase your awareness of colleagues' perceptions?

◆ How can you increase your awareness of the details of your performance?

## PERSONAL DEVELOPMENT

Assessment of both positive and negative leadership behavior provides a basis for improved performance. Even so, any change in behavior is best made so that it builds upon qualities that leaders already possess and enhances their existing leadership style. Everyone has a unique personality made up of a blend of qualities, such as courage, patience, ambition, honesty, and others.

The more recognized these qualities are, the more easily a leader can draw upon them with confidence. This also leads to discovery of which qualities leaders lack. With this information a leader can decide what needs to be developed and therefore how future performance can be improved.

For example, an inability to give clear directions is a negative leadership behavior with a variety of potential causes. A leader benefits from examining his or her personal qualities to determine the specific source of the difficulty. Does this leader need better preparation, more poise, tighter thinking, or improved judgment? An identical problem could require a variety of remedies depending upon each individual's blend of qualities.

## Positive behavior

The first task is to identify this blend of individual qualities. The two lists of positive behavior, drawn from personal and colleagues' points of view, aids this process. Each item on the lists potentially leads to identification of a personal quality.

For example, one item may read: "Remained calm during a crisis." This behavior could result from a variety of qualities, such as courage, steadiness, or trust. When individuals recognize which quality is at the source of their calm, they can draw upon this consciously on future occasions. This insight has direct benefit for the development of self-confidence. "I am calm in a crisis because I have courage." This thought obviously enhances self-image. It also stabilizes performance, because the quality is one that the individual already possesses.

Once a quality is identified for each item on the list, it is useful to write it next to that item. Some qualities may be repeated and others may offer a surprise. The point is that each feature of behavior is drawn from a personal quality that in turn contributes to leadership performance. Frequently, this is difficult to believe or accept if these qualities have been criticized in the past.

For example, potential leaders who express gentleness or humility are not always understood. Rather than suppress these qualities, leaders need to learn how to present them so that they enhance their performance. This is *always* possible, and the process begins with self-acceptance and a determination to explore how best to express each quality. Personal development means building upon existing strengths and managing weaknesses. Masking or hiding personal qualities creates good actors, not good leaders.

### Negative behavior
Negative comments provide further opportunity for growth. Through newly developed awareness, leaders can choose to change

their behavior. For example, if a leader is criticized for using humor when presenting official company business to a department, this creates the possibility for choice. Options include: that a sense of humor is not an appropriate leadership quality; that rebellion against the criticism and increased use of humor is best; or that learning can be gained from the comment by discovering exactly what it means. Rather than react blindly, this individual can choose to analyze and grow.

On receiving negative feedback, leaders should ask:

◆ Did I really do what this person says I did?

◆ Does this person have all the facts?

◆ On reflection, do I believe my behavior was appropriate to all three essentials: time, place, and audience?

◆ If not, when, where, and with whom is it appropriate to express this quality in this way?

## Improving behavior

Leaders who manage themselves effectively enhance their skills when leading others. Both positive and negative feedback offers valuable information and helps leaders learn how behavior impacts on supporters. The lists of both positive and negative behavior can be used to identify personal qualities. Negative items offer further benefit because they draw attention to specific behavior that needs improvement.

In general, these items can be organized into three areas for development. These are: skills, knowledge, and experience. On reviewing the lists of negative features, it can be asked of each item, "Was this behavior the result of a lack of skill, knowledge, or experience?" Three lists can thus be compiled:

1. *Skills*: List items that reveal a need for new skill.

2. *Knowledge*: List items that reveal a need for further knowledge.

3. *Experience*: List items that reveal a need for more experience.

## Plan of action

Developing skills, knowledge, and experience strengthens the weak areas in leadership. Review the previous list of categorized features and decide which skills, knowledge, and experience are necessary for leadership development, and then compile three lists:

1. new skills

2. new knowledge

3. new experience

Next, consider how this development can be achieved in each of these three areas. Set one specific goal for each area:

1. a goal for skills

2. a goal for knowledge

3. a goal for experience

Later, when these goals are achieved, the list can be reviewed again to set new goals for improving skills, knowledge, and experience.

*Checklist*

◆ Think of one occasion during the day when you took the lead.

◆ Describe this in one or two sentences.

◆ What qualities did you express?

◆ What challenges did you experience?

◆ What do you like about your performance?

◆ What can you do to improve your performance?

# Chapter 2

## Understanding People

The second step to successful leadership is understanding people. This emphasizes the importance of recognizing individual differences in terms of drives, dreams, and ambitions. Leaders must beware of the belief that everyone is really the same. They are not, and it is not democratic to insist that they are. Differences, not similarities, make groups strong and life interesting. When individuals are lumped together as "the same," they are deprived of their independence and individuality.

Topics that are relevant to the development of this theme are

◆ motivation.

◆ rewards and values.

◆ inspiration.

## MOTIVATION

Before the study of psychology gained social acceptance during this century, leaders generally kept silent about any feelings of self-doubt. Instead, they presented the world with an image of strength and determination and the appearance of complete confidence regardless of their inner state. The leader's task was to motivate others through his example. Self-questioning was perceived to be the habit of weaklings. It even implied disloyalty and a lack of commitment to the position as leader.

Strength, determination, and confidence continue to be valued leadership qualities. Even so, it is generally accepted now that leaders also experience a wide range of emotions and are driven by a variety of motives, some of which are positive and some negative. In fact, it is now considered a weakness to pose as the perfect and all-knowing leader. It is a strength to recognize and even admit the experience of fear in order to understand, address, and overcome it.

Managing such negative as well as positive feelings requires an understanding of human motivation. Current thinking on this subject suggests that individuals are motivated to satisfy different needs at different times. Their first requirement is to meet their basic survival needs. Only when these are satisfied are they able to work towards achieving growth and creating meaning in their lives. It is the drive to fulfill needs for survival and growth that leads them to overcome feelings of fear and other limitations.

One pioneer in the study of human motivation is Abraham Maslow. He proposed that there is a hierarchy of needs with five different levels. As individuals satisfy all of the needs on each of these levels, they are then naturally motivated to progress and satisfy the needs on the next level. The hierarchy of needs suggests that human motivation is similar to the force that plants use to force their roots through the hardest rock in search of nourishment. The hierarchy of needs is generally presented in the form of a pyramid as shown here.

This model suggests that motivation develops in a sequence. When the immediate needs for food, clothing, and shelter are met, then individuals use their energy to ensure that their physical safety and comfort are secure in the future as well. Having satisfied these first two basic survival needs, they then give their full attention to building friendships and family relationships.

As soon as the need for belonging is satisfied, individuals then strive for a sense of personal achievement and an experience of self-esteem. Achieving satisfaction of all four of these need levels allows them to examine the purpose and meaning of their work and lives. Essentially, this means that people who are hungry and without shelter give their primary attention to satisfying these needs before they feel willing or able to discuss philosophy.

These unsatisfied needs dominate behavior. For example, a colleague who is under stress about money or is in poor health brings less attention to team relationships and certainly has impaired creativity. Even if leaders are powerless to alter their colleagues' circumstances, they can show sensitivity when discussing the impaired performance.

This basic understanding of the impact of needs on motivation and performance is vital for effective leadership. It is the key to knowing how to play to colleagues' strengths and to help them overcome their weaknesses.

Motivation is never uniform throughout a whole team. A leader encourages team members to want to achieve a vision by recognizing *each individual's* starting point and building upon this. Inspirational speeches to the whole of the group at one extreme and punishment threats at the other have only a temporary influence on performance. Those measures that serve everyone in the long term focus on individual colleagues' driving concerns and issues. Satisfaction of these needs contributes directly to improved performance for the group.

## Leadership practice

These checklists serve as a guide for applying the hierarchy of needs to understanding colleagues' motivation.

Think of a colleague with whom you work. What kinds of needs does this person discuss most?

◆ physical comforts?

◆ job security?

◆ friends, family, social events?

◆ job satisfaction, recognition, status?

◆ values, principles, quality work for its own sake?

How does this person respond when issues related to each level of need are raised?

◆ easily and naturally?

◆ with a lack of comprehension?

◆ with impatience or cynicism?

If *easily and naturally*, needs are likely to be satisfied on the level being discussed as well as on the level below it.

If *lacking in comprehension*, it is likely that attention is focused more on satisfying needs on the level below.

If *impatiently and cynically*, needs are unlikely to be satisfied on this level or on the level below it. This has an impact on the person's overall ability to find satisfaction at work. Their motivation is affected because they assume they will be disappointed by what they receive.

## Leadership solutions

When leaders understand the frustrations and limitations of their colleagues, they are better able *to present a vision so that others want to achieve it*. For example, when presenting the benefits of a quality improvement program, it is ineffective to emphasize the importance of quality for its own sake when colleagues are primarily worried about losing their jobs.

Leaders who give proper attention to their colleagues' needs take time to explain that the quality program not only benefits the company, but also contributes to each employee's work satisfaction, teamwork, job security, and physical well-being. Addressing colleagues' concerns in this way shows respect for their needs and leads to increased motivation.

## REWARDS AND VALUES

During infancy and childhood, individuals form patterns of behavior that ensure their survival. For example, some babies scream, cry, and demand food and other essentials. Others babble, coo, and charm their parents into giving them what they need. A third group simply learns that they are on their own and must expect the bare minimum from other people. Although actual behavior changes with maturity, the underlying patterns remain in place.

These patterns of behavior form three categories. It is suggested that individuals develop a strategy to obtain what they need by using one of these patterns.

*Individuals are*

◆ ambitious and assertive.

◆ caring and supportive.

◆ analytic and cautious.

Each of these orientations is deeply embedded in an individual's makeup. These patterns are often so strong that individuals behave as if they had no choice. Frequently, they are on automatic pilot and are unaware of how they are behaving until a colleague comments on it.

Even when leaders clearly explain that there are options, habits of mind and behavior route the individual into behaving according to past patterns. Not only should leaders be aware of the nature of their personal pattern but they should also encourage colleagues to be more self-aware, particularly when their behavior affects other people.

## Ambitious and assertive

Ambitious and assertive individuals frequently have more ideas than there are hours in the day to achieve them. They are driven by a need to make their mark on the world. The leader's task is to remind them of the group's priorities. If a leader can also recognize their level of motivation, then tasks can be presented to them so that they gain their full attention. This category of behavior is an extremely challenging one to manage. Even so, when these individuals feel motivated to complete a task, nothing stops them.

## Caring and supportive

Although the warmth and friendliness of these colleagues are certainly virtues, frequently they actually result from habit and a desire to please and be liked. Even so, they are a positive force in any group because they truly enjoy giving support. In fact, these individuals feel most rewarded when their help is accepted. The leader's task is to guide these colleagues into being more independent. They also need to be reassured when the loners of the group refuse their support.

## Analytic and cautious

Analytic and cautious colleagues feel most satisfied when they work alone. They enjoy the solitude, the concentration, and the sense of independence this gives them. For them to achieve a task is a reward in itself. For example, these individuals genuinely feel burdened when asked to attend an office party because it interferes with their work.

Properly managed, this pattern of behavior is a valuable asset to the team. Unhappily, these loners often find themselves with well-meaning leaders who are determined to help them "overcome their shyness."

There are positive and negative features of each pattern:

## Ambitious and assertive

| *Positive features* | *Negative features* |
| --- | --- |
| ◆ confident | ◆ arrogant |
| ◆ dynamic | ◆ pushy |
| ◆ risk-taking | ◆ gambling |
| ◆ spontaneous | ◆ impulsive |
| ◆ directing | ◆ dictatorial |
| ◆ entrepreneurial | ◆ uncooperative |
| ◆ resourceful | ◆ calculating |

## Caring and supportive

| *Positive features* | *Negative features* |
| --- | --- |
| ◆ sensitive | ◆ high strung |
| ◆ devoted | ◆ doormat |
| ◆ idealistic | ◆ deluded |
| ◆ friendly | ◆ naïve |
| ◆ tolerant | ◆ blind |
| ◆ patient | ◆ passive |
| ◆ understanding | ◆ submissive |

## Analytic and cautious

| *Positive features* | *Negative features* |
|---|---|
| ◆ practical | ◆ narrow-minded |
| ◆ independent | ◆ self-serving |
| ◆ fair | ◆ impersonal |
| ◆ thorough | ◆ nit-picking |
| ◆ reserved | ◆ isolated |
| ◆ methodical | ◆ plodding |
| ◆ principled | ◆ rigid |

## INSPIRATION

The creation of positive relationships and mutual respect is a major source of inspiration for both leaders and followers.

A sense of shared understanding provides a basis for strong relationships. The leaders' task is to create bonds of mutual respect between themselves and their supporters. However, there are still leaders who believe that it is necessary to set themselves apart from their followers. They believe that they need a mystique that is based upon their being different, smarter, or better than their colleagues. They see this as their source of power.

Even 50 years ago this would have been considered conventional leadership behavior, and yet currently it is not generally accepted as appropriate. There has been an explosion of information technology and telecommunications that subtly alter the way individuals relate to each other within their organizations. Also, the average person is better educated and more sophisticated than the majority enerations. As a result, leaders are now required to and information with greater flexibility and skill

...........leadership has always depended upon communication skills, both listening and speaking. There is now an additional need to use these skills to build interdependent relationships within the group and between the leaders and their supporters. This doesn't dilute the role of leader; rather it adds new challenges.

In fact, it has always been a requirement of leaders to relate well to followers. History's greatest leaders show consistent evidence of this. These figures recognized that their authority and power emerged from their supporters.

The respect they gave their colleagues directly led to receipt of both loyalty and commitment.

*Checklist*

◆ Think of one occasion during the day in which you took the lead.

◆ Describe this in one or two sentences.

◆ What did you want to achieve?

◆ Were there any personal needs that you could satisfy through leading?

◆ Were you aware of your colleagues' motivation?

◆ Did you consider their needs?

◆ Did your approach reflect a style that was ambitious and assertive, caring and supportive, or analytic and cautious?

# Chapter 3

## Power and Authority

The third step to successful leadership emphasizes the importance of understanding power and authority. When individuals accept the responsibility of leadership, they also assume the challenge of managing power wisely and for the benefit of their whole group. This chapter explores topics that concern the proper exercise of power and authority:

◆ managing power

◆ styles of leadership

◆ adapting to events

◆ delegation

## MANAGING POWER

The title *leader* does not in itself create leadership; there must also be a positive relationship with those who are led. Discussion, feedback, and debate are essential so that a leader can *learn* from other members of the group. Repressing, ignoring, or discouraging different points of view within a group is a sign of a weak and frightened leader who must hide behind a role in order to control the group.

At the heart of much of the debate about leadership style is the issue:

*When leaders ask their colleagues for feedback, comments, and advice, do they undermine or weaken their own authority?*

Most definitely, they do *not*. Every leader potentially can be undermined, manipulated, or overthrown. These hazards result more often from an *unwillingness to allow debate*, not from an openness to encourage it. Confidence, curiosity, and tolerance are qualities of strong leadership. Inevitably, the leader who possesses these positive traits stimulates debate.

Only when everyone has had an opportunity to speak, does this leader recognize that it is time to bring the discussion to a close. A genuine interest in hearing colleagues' points of view and an open invitation to debate key issues is the mark of a powerful and confident leader, not a weak one.

Unfortunately, power is so often abused that for many it has become a dirty word. Even so, leaders who manage power effectively serve their organizations, colleagues, and themselves. It is far better for those who have integrity and character to have leadership power than those who show a history of its abuse.

There are four kinds of power:

◆ designated

◆ expert

◆ charismatic

◆ information

Each contributes to successful leadership.

## Designated power

This kind of power depends upon a specific and formally recognized organizational role. Individuals with this power are officially appointed to act on behalf of their organizations. When the role is left behind, the leader gives up the power associated with that role.

This means that a department head who is transferred to another position no longer has the power to lead that department. It passes to the next designated leader. On occasion, some leaders try to hang on to this kind of power; this behavior creates considerable bad feeling and can never be successful.

## Expert power

This kind of power depends upon the personal talents, skills, and experience of the individuals who possess it. They have this power regardless of their official role within an organization. Some leaders have both designated and expert power and find this an extremely challenging experience.

Frequently, the demands of a designated leadership role inhibit the development of the *highest* degree of expertise in a given field. This causes some specialists to avoid designated positions. Often, expert power is exerted informally. Effective leaders should identify those individuals with expert power because their contribution to the group is often as important as those in designated positions.

## Charismatic power

Those who have charismatic power possess both a blessing and a curse. They are frequently the wild cards in any organization. Historically, highly charismatic leaders tend to end up in disgrace, alone, in prison, or in Hollywood!

Even so, a charismatic leader can inspire colleagues to want to give their best, at least for a time. It is therefore tempting for those leaders to depend upon this source of power as their sole source of influence. This is not wise. To ensure that there is substance behind their charm and dazzle, leaders should draw on other sources of power *along with* charisma to influence events.

## Information power

This source of power has gained increasing importance because new electronic technology now allows the management of vast amounts of information. In the past, organizations depended upon long-serving members as sources of information power. Human memory provided access to information that was vital and necessary for running the company. This is now more frequently available through electronic systems.

Because a lack of information at critical junctures is potentially catastrophic, this kind of power is best managed through sharing the responsibility for storing information. In this way, the organization avoids dependence upon single individuals and isolated electronic systems as sources of information power.

## Integration

When leaders draw on more than one source of power, they strengthen their position. Exercising authority and influencing results becomes easier when the individual's source of power is obvious and is recognized immediately. There is a danger, of course, because it is very difficult to challenge a leader who draws authority from all four sources of power. On occasion even such a paragon will be wrong. This is reason enough to avoid leadership that is isolated or surrounded by yes-saying admirers. Doing so is but a minimal safeguard against the mistaken use of power.

*Activity*

◆ Think of examples for all four kinds of power that you have observed.

◆ Consider specific occasions when you have exercised each of these four kinds of power.

◆ Was there any occasion when you chose to exercise the wrong kind of power (e.g., you overwhelmed colleagues with data when your task was to lead a meeting)?

◆ If you could relive this event, how would you manage power differently?

## STYLES OF LEADERSHIP

Power and authority are expressed through a style of leadership. There are three basic styles:

◆ democratic

◆ autocratic

◆ permissive

### Democratic

There are leaders who feel constantly frustrated because they are surrounded by witless underlings rather than peers. Even when they engage new people, these too gradually reveal their weakness. Such leaders are actually in serious trouble. When the whole world begins to look wrong, it is time to improve the viewer, not the viewed.

In contrast, a democratic style of leadership is based upon mutual respect among colleagues regardless of designated positions. When these leaders discover that their colleagues lack certain skills and abilities, they create opportunities for them to grow and develop. The strength of this style is the atmosphere of discussion and debate that it encourages.

Everyone gains from this, including the leaders who are challenged to learn from their colleagues. There are few more satisfying leadership achievements than to gather a group of moderately skilled and underdeveloped colleagues and then, through working together, to create a team of individually powerful and dynamic peers.

## Autocratic

This style of leadership often appears to be most beneficial whenever there is controversy. Confused individuals long for a strong boss, a leader who will tell them what to do.

Certainly, there are enough historical examples of autocratic dictators who were *invited* into power to show that some people value this style of leadership very much.

Even so, there is strong research evidence that groups with a single, order-giving leader have poorer productivity and performance as well as greater discontent than those who are led democratically. When leaders are too frightened, too proud, or too conceited to open a discussion among their colleagues, they actually undermine their own authority. They have lost an opportunity to demonstrate their confidence, judgment, and willingness to learn.

## Permissive

The permissive style is frequently a misguided attempt at democracy. The individual who exercises this style of leadership is often well-meaning and reluctant to impose his or her will on other people.

Unfortunately, these virtues can be infuriating to other people whose work requires coordination, active support, and direction.

The permissive leader frequently does not realize that giving guidance and acting as a forceful champion for the group is part of the leader's job. Although colleagues often like these nice guy leaders—both male and female—they also describe them as weak, spineless, and incompetent, regretting the day that they began working for them.

All three styles are both potentially beneficial and potentially frustrating to group members.

*Frustrations*

◆ *Democratic*: These leaders drive action-first colleagues crazy because discussion takes time and slows progress.

◆ *Autocratic*: These leaders are so one-sided that they infuriate colleagues who want to contribute ideas and information.

◆ *Permissive*: These leaders force their colleagues to accept inactivity through lack of direction and guidance.

*Benefits*

◆ *Democratic*: These leaders encourage everyone to contribute skills and talents so that more work of a higher quality gets done.

◆ *Autocratic*: These leaders offer speed, single-mindedness, and clarity when firm direction is required; on occasion a team actually benefits from being told what to do.

◆ *Permissive*: These leaders serve highly creative people who respond well to a structure-free environment. This style is useful when little group coordination is required.

## ADAPTING TO EVENTS

Effective leaders are flexible when deciding which leadership style is the best one for their group at any given time. They determine this by considering the *stage of development* of their group. Two leading figures in the field of management study, Paul Hersey and Ken Blanchard, suggest that there are four distinct stages in the development of every group.

The *first stage* begins when the group first forms. The leader's role at this point should be directive so that the project gets under way. Once group members know their assignments and have clear directions, the leader next encourages them to get to know each other better. This builds strong group relationships and is the *second stage* of group development.

In the *third stage,* the leader emphasizes the importance of members sharing responsibility and discussing the project's needs. In this way they gradually develop an awareness of their interdependence. In the *fourth stage,* the leader functions merely as a guide and coach to members, who begin to run the project themselves. They have grown into a mature group.

This four-stage model is very useful when deciding which kind of leadership style is best for a group. It also helps explain why a group on occasion seems to benefit from being told what to do and at other times seems to resent it.

It is important to emphasize that the successful use of this model depends upon a leader's ability to assess a group's stage of development. An obvious challenge arises for the autocratic leader whose behavior keeps the group from developing beyond stage one. This individual can easily argue that the model recommends directing and controlling activities because the group is so immature.

## DELEGATION

The issue of group maturity can be resolved in part if leaders also learn skills of delegation. There are four stages to this process as well. These are:

**1.** Define the task.

**2.** Show why it is important.

**3.** Explain any expectations.

**4.** Evaluate and discuss results.

## STAGE 1
*Define the task*

This is so obvious a step that it is often given little attention. Instead, an assignment is simply handed to a colleague who is then asked to get it done. Leaders who want to ensure more reliable results take time to discuss the task in some detail. They also ask the colleague to go through the key points of the assignment to uncover questions.

This highlights any gaps in that person's understanding and encourages comments and new ideas for the task's successful completion. This approach is essential to create *empowerment*, that is, encouraging a colleague to share in the responsibility for the task's completion and success. Inviting a discussion about the task when it is first assigned evokes a colleague's interest and stimulates commitment.

## STAGE 2
*Show why it is important*

Adults perform at their best when they see the relevance of what they are doing. They need a larger context in which to place a task or a project. This also contributes to their feeling of empowerment. When they know the significance of the task they have been asked to perform, they can make better decisions about its completion and reduce their mistakes. Employees appreciate information about context. It is a sign that the leader takes them seriously.

## STAGE 3
*Explain any expectations*

If colleagues do not know what is expected of them, they cannot possibly meet a leader's expectations. When delegating it is essential to explain when and how they will be evaluated. People also need to know in advance any limitations upon their authority for completion of the task. Leaders who *say* that they give complete authority with the task cannot be surprised if this offer is accepted. Colleagues are not mind readers. They cannot guess limits, even if these limits are completely obvious to the person delegating the task.

## STAGE 4
*Evaluate and discuss results*

This step builds upon the previous one. When expectations are explained in advance, then colleagues have clear performance goals towards which to work. When a leader reveals performance criteria only after a task is complete, this causes unnecessary hurt and disappointment. It is impossible to meet invisible or secret targets.

Keeping colleagues guessing is a leadership technique that belongs to the dark ages. There is no fairness in such a system of evaluation and it certainly undermines motivation for task completion. In essence, it is power mongering, however cheerily or reasonably it is justified.

*Checklist*

◆ Think of one occasion during the day when you took the lead.

◆ Describe this in one or two sentences.

◆ What kind of power did you exercise?

◆ What alternative kinds of power would also have served this situation?

◆ What style of leadership did you use?

◆ How did your colleagues respond to your leadership?

◆ What stage of development has your group achieved?

◆ Were there any tasks that you could have delegated today but did not?

# Chapter 4

## Communication

All work and social exchange depends upon communication. It is the means for sharing ideas, feelings, and resources. When communication breaks down, disagreements and misunderstandings immediately occur. Even so, communication skills are frequently taken for granted.

It is assumed that colleagues who speak the same language need only time, effort, and sincerity to communicate successfully. This optimistic view ignores the impact of emotions, motivation, intelligence, risk taking, and competition, among many other issues. For this reason, communication is the fourth step to successful leadership. This chapter looks at these essential components of effective communication:

◆ listening and speaking

◆ social skills

◆ creating understanding

## LISTENING AND SPEAKING

Communication is based upon giving and receiving information. In its simplest form, this consists of two activities: listening and speaking. In fact, both of these require highly complex behavior and draw upon each person's lifetime of experience.

Even a brief encounter consisting of only a casual greeting is the result of years of practice. Through trial and error over the passage of time, individuals create a personal style of greeting. They become so skilled that they also know how to adapt this to meet the changing needs of each situation.

### Listening

Listening requires a leader to be aware of three essential features: bias, visual signals, and vocal sounds.

### FEATURE 1
*Bias*

Everyone's point of view includes some bias even if they are not entirely conscious of it. Bias refers to thinking that is either in favor of or against a person, event, or idea. It reflects an individual's ability to understand and interpret correctly what he sees and hears. It is difficult to determine the extent to which bias undermines good judgment or the ability to hear accurately what is said.

Bias is a problem when it seriously distorts an individual's understanding. It becomes dangerous when it also limits an ability to accept that it even exists or could have a negative influence. One result of bias is the exclusion of information whose source is unattractive or in some way different from the listener.

Indicators of bias include extreme reactions to people or situations, either in favor or against; paying attention only to the parts of a presentation that are already understood; or assuming an understanding of what is said before a statement is even concluded.

## FEATURE 2
*Visual signals*

A visual signal is body language. There are many seminars and books available that offer interpretations of commonly used gestures and signs. These often represent a sincere effort to improve understanding and communication. In a multicultural society, it should also be emphasized that gestures carry a wide variety of meanings for different cultural groups.

People interpret the meaning of body language according to their own understanding. A population with diverse backgrounds and nationalities lacks a common meaning for the symbols contained in visual language. Therefore, it is unwise to make generalizations about a single meaning for certain signs and gestures as if there were a universal code available.

Even so, gestures add considerable meaning to communication. Listening is obviously enhanced when both eyes and ears are used simultaneously. The difficulty is assuming that there is an understanding when there is a possibility of doubt. If a speaker depends upon ambiguous gestures, then it is important to ask what these mean. An incorrect interpretation of visual signals can lead to serious misunderstanding.

## FEATURE 3
*Vocal sounds*

Listening to the sound and tone of a speaker's voice enhances understanding. Sometimes there are hidden messages that can be captured with careful listening. For example, speakers signal their emotional state as well as an attitude towards their audience through their voice. At times, it is more important to hear these subtle messages than the actual content of what is said. If a speaker's tone of voice contrasts with the actual spoken message, then a listener should ask for clarification. Although this requires tact, it contributes to improved understanding.

*Activity*

◆ During the day, observe at least three conversations between people you do not know.

Conversation one: Bias

◆ Do you imagine that there is any bias between these people?

◆ What causes you to think this?

◆ If you were engaged in this conversation, would you feel bias?

◆ What form would this take?

◆ What could you do about your bias in order to improve understanding?

Conversation two: Visual signals

◆ Do these people seem to share a cultural background?

◆ Are they using similar gestures and facial expressions?

◆ How and when are these signals used?

◆ Do you understand their significance?

◆ How do you know that you understand?

◆ What could you do to improve your ability to interpret these visual signals?

Conversation three: Vocal sounds

◆ Does the tone of voice match the content of what is being said?

◆ Do both speakers use the same voice tone and volume?

◆ Do they seem aware of the impact of their voice tone?

◆ If you joined this conversation, would you use a similar tone of voice?

◆ What could you do to become more conscious of the effect of your voice on others?

## Speaking

From the lightest social conversation to the most challenging business exchange, speaking requires an ordered and logical presentation of thoughts. Although much speaking ability is taken for granted, its success depends upon preparation. In many cases, this preparation is so rapidly achieved that speaking occurs simultaneously with an individual planning what is to be said.

This style is called "flying by the seat of your pants," "thinking on your feet," or "winging it." Much is left to chance when speakers depend solely upon this approach. The best speakers use techniques that make listening to them an easy and positive experience. These techniques include: headlining, pacing, and summarizing.

## Headlining

Just as a news headline signals a story's main ideas, speakers can highlight their key thoughts in their opening sentence. They begin by stating clearly what they want to discuss and then expanding upon this initial idea. When each main thought is completed, they then give another headline. This approach avoids listeners having to ask: "What is the point?" If this has *ever* happened to a speaker, even once, then this technique is a useful one to develop.

## Pacing

Good speakers attend to the needs of their audience. Pacing refers to the ability to stop talking and invite listeners to comment. Sadly, some speakers believe that their turn to speak is over only when they have expressed every one of their ideas. Too often this also means exhausting their audience as well.

An alternative approach suggests that a speaker pauses when presentation of each headline is complete. The listener then responds or offers a new headline. Both speakers and listeners contribute and participate equally when using this approach.

Pacing also refers to a speaker's ability to create interest by slowing and speeding up delivery of a message. Speakers who use a single tone of voice without changing its rhythm are less engaging than those with a more variable style.

## Summarizing

"I tell them what I plan to say; then I tell them; then I tell them what I just said." This is the age-old wisdom for report writing and public speaking. The approach is not entirely suitable for everyday conversation, but it does highlight the importance of summarizing key ideas. Gathering several headlined ideas into a summary adds structure to a communication. It signals that there is mutual understanding—or at least that certain points have been discussed and are complete.

*Activity*

◆ During three separate conversations, practice these three techniques.

Conversation one: Headlining

◆ Before speaking, capture your main thought in a headline.

◆ Begin by stating the headline clearly and briefly.

◆ Continue speaking so that you expand upon this headline *only*.

◆ If other related issues emerge, make headlines for each of these.

◆ Be aware of moving from one headline to another.

Conversation two: Pacing

◆ Listen and identify the pace of the other person.

◆ As you speak, notice if your pace is different.

◆ Alter your pace if you can without losing the thread of what you are saying.

◆ Be aware of the signals you use to show that you have finished speaking.

◆ Be aware of the signals the other person uses to show a wish to speak.

Conversation three: Summarizing

◆ When you complete a headline, paraphrase what has been said.

◆ After several contributions by both speakers, highlight key points.

◆ When the discussion has slowed, make a clear statement of its conclusions so far.

◆ At the end of the conversation, list all of the headlines that were covered.

## SOCIAL SKILLS

Listening and speaking form the foundations of communication. They both contribute in equal measure to the development of socially skilled information exchange. Researchers highlight five essential features of clear and effective communication and refer to them as social skills. Socially skilled communication is:

◆ goal directed

◆ coherent

◆ appropriate to the situation

◆ controlled

◆ able to be learned

## Goal directed

When there are clear goals for the exchange of ideas or information, it is easier to recognize when communication is complete. Discussion is far more satisfying when participants have something they wish to achieve through communication because they can then work to accomplish this.

Telling a joke is an excellent example of goal-directed communication. The narrator knows the communication is a success when the listener starts to laugh.

Taking time to consider the purpose of sharing information influences the choice of words and contributes to a more confident presentation.

## Coherent

This refers to behavior that makes a single, consistent, overall impression as well as to the clarity and logic of the message. For example, when presenting serious information that could alarm a listener, a socially skilled speaker controls eye contact, facial expression, tone of voice, and body language so that they blend to give a single message. Nervous smiling or a hesitating manner when information is urgent detracts from the speaker's credibility and potentially distorts the message.

## Appropriate to the situation

Socially skilled communication coordinates words, behavior, and timing so that presentation of information matches the needs of the situation. While coherence refers specifically to *personal style* when delivering a message, this additional skill requires thinking about when and how a message is best delivered. This means choosing the right method, such as telephone, handwritten note, electronic means, or face-to-face speech. One example of this social skill is a leader who criticizes a colleague face to face in private rather than in a public place.

## Controlled

This social skill refers to the leader's self-discipline rather than the ability to discipline others. On occasion, leaders make decisions that benefit the group rather than reflect their personal preference.

An example of this kind of behavior is the leader who resists taking over a task once it has been delegated. It takes enormous control to watch a less-experienced colleague struggle to learn a task that the leader could complete in just a few minutes. The reward for this kind of self-control is a stronger team.

## Able to be learned

The ability to learn how to communicate is a vital social skill. Unfortunately, most communication behavior is learned by absorption and copying rather than by conscious choice. A speaker's voice, gestures, and movement are the result of a lifetime of conditioning. Leaders serve themselves and their colleagues when they evaluate their own communication skills in order to learn what and how they can improve.

This learning process is aided by examining the strength of the other four social skills: the ability to set a goal for discussion; to be coherent; to time the delivery of information; and to maintain self-control. If any of these skills is weak, then leaders need to focus attention on social skill development.

*Preparation for an important communication*

◆ What are your goals for this occasion, both personal and professional?

◆ Does your style of dress, choice of language, and tone of voice make a single, harmonious impression?

◆ Is the timing and choice of method right for the delivery of your message?

◆ Are you as fully prepared to listen to others as you are to speak?

◆ What do you plan to learn from this experience?

## CREATING UNDERSTANDING

It is the leader's responsibility to open a debate, encourage colleagues' contributions, and guide discussion so that a common understanding emerges within the group. This understanding enhances a group's sense of purpose and contributes to their sense of unity.

Opening a discussion that addresses difficult issues offers an enormous challenge. Some leaders just give up at the first sign of dissent or confusion. They begin to bark orders and silence discussion out of fear of losing control. If they could develop the courage to persevere, they would reap enormous rewards.

When leaders are committed to creating understanding, they show this through attentive listening and setting a tone of tolerant discussion within the group. Not only do these leaders gain benefit from their colleagues' ideas, they also encourage group loyalty and commitment. It has already been suggested that respect generates respect. The leader has the power to begin this positive spiral of mutual appreciation.

The key task is to achieve a balance between creative contribution and opinion free-for-all, where the loudest voice gets heard most. To avoid anarchy while also fostering debate requires a leader to set and follow ground rules for the discussion. These ensure that everyone's ideas receive a fair hearing. The leader assumes the role of discussion moderator. This is a difficult task, although skilled practitioners make it look very easy. The goal is to encourage a free exchange among all and avoid domination by just a few.

Discussion skills include:

◆ coaching

◆ paraphrasing

◆ intervention

## Coaching

An essential leadership task is to state the purpose for the discussion at the beginning. If this is an open debate, then one person must not be allowed to hold forth and dominate. To avoid this as the discussion begins, the leader should announce that people should speak one at a time and wait to be acknowledged for their turn.

As the discussion continues, the leader watches who in the group wants to speak. A system of turn taking should be followed during even an informal gathering. Some leaders fail to monitor discussion in this way, arguing that they want to avoid controlling the debate. As a result, some participants speak up when they wish and others hold back or are spoken over. Forced silence creates frustration.

This is always unsatisfactory and allows the loudest and most confident to control the discussion. It is better to risk insisting that forceful members wait for acknowledgement than to ignore the quiet participants. A fair leadership style during discussion earns everyone's respect and encourages full participation. Even highly vocal members eventually appreciate fairness.

## Paraphrasing

If the discussion digresses from the main point, paraphrasing allows the leader to bring it back on track. This requires repeating the key ideas of the side topic in a paraphrase and then restating what has been covered on the main topic. This is best accomplished in a nonjudgmental manner.

If leaders catch digression quickly, they avoid feelings of frustration themselves and can more easily reaffirm the main topic without showing any strain. Those who began the digression can be invited to raise their points again when the main topic has been covered.

## Intervention

When two or more participants are locked in a dispute, they need encouragement to pause and take a step back from their positions. This is so that they can gain a new perspective. Often it helps to ask the other participants to speak *on the same issue*. If a new voice takes this opportunity to raise a different topic, the leader should gently insist on staying with the controversial issue. A change of topic leads to continuation of a dispute rather than resolution.

Occasionally, a well-meaning participant tries to change the discussion topic as a way of avoiding controversy. Skillful intervention can prevent this. The leader's task is to take attention away from the disputing *participants* and focus on the *issues* they raised. The next step is to encourage the rest of the group to discuss the controversial issues and seek a solution.

*Checklist*

◆ What did you learn from the observed conversations by focusing on listening?

◆ What did you learn from the observed conversations by focusing on speaking?

◆ Think of an occasion during the day when you took the lead.

◆ Describe this in one or two sentences.

◆ Did you have a goal, either personal or professional, for your communication?

◆ How do you rate your performance in terms of:
  – coherence?
  – appropriateness?
  – self-control?

◆ At any time during the day, did you lead a group discussion?

◆ If so, how do you rate your ability to:
  – coach?
  – paraphrase?
  – intervene?

# Chapter 5

## Decision Making

The fifth step to successful leadership is decision making. Whether a leader does this alone or within a group, it is essential that supporters see their leader act with confidence on their behalf. When the discussion of a decision is complete, it is the leader who signals that it is time to take action. Decision-making skills are improved by focusing on these issues:

◆ identifying priorities

◆ setting clear goals

◆ using a systematic approach

## WHAT ARE PRIORITIES?

Frequently, leaders are required to make several decisions at the same time. Because full attention cannot be given to each issue simultaneously, they need to coordinate and manage information with considerable skill. There are also added distractions because many of their decisions have unforeseen impact upon other matters. Decision makers must determine the extent of interdependence among a variety of issues even as they are estimating their degree of importance.

This requires identifying priorities and making decisions about the most pressing issues first. This takes discipline, because some decisions appear to require immediate attention and yet lack genuine urgency or importance for the long term. In contrast, some truly vital issues are forgotten because they lack glamor or noisy advocates to press for their attention.

> *Priorities have two features:* urgency *and* importance. *The leader's task is to identify these and act upon them.*

Complications also occur when identified priority issues spill over into other business areas. Leaders are then required to make further decisions even while coordinating previously identified priorities. With practice, this juggling act of managing priorities and making timely decisions becomes a routine performance.

The process of acquiring these skills begins with knowing how to recognize priorities. Only then can leaders manage their impact on these related issues. Confusion can arise because some tasks are urgent and yet of only short-term relevance. For example, assigning a staff member to give a group of school children a tour of the building is of limited relevance to the business. Even so, it is an urgent matter if the school children are standing in the cold waiting to be invited indoors.

## Two criteria

When prioritizing decisions, it is useful to separate issues into "future important" and "current urgent." Some decisions fit neither category at the time while others fit both. A few urgent decisions are also highly important because they provide a basis for future decisions. For example, a deadline for action gives urgency to the decision to file a request to the town council for planning permission. Although the actual decision to fill in the form is a minor one, it has long-term importance as well because it marks the first step for major decision making later.

Priority setting begins by examining all of the decisions that are currently required of the leader and the group. These can be listed in preparation for discussion by the whole group or for study by individuals or a small working party.

To illustrate this, the manager of a 10-member human resources department reviews several forthcoming decisions. These could include office refurbishment, vacation schedules, staff allocation for new projects, and a new insurance benefits package proposed by the company's personnel officer.

Each of these main issues includes sub-tasks that will contribute to completion of the larger task. Even so, the manager wants to avoid getting drawn into considering these before assessing the urgency and importance of the four main topics. Time is particularly tight for this leader and so knowing which decisions are both urgent and important is essential. By setting priorities, decision-making time can be better managed.

The four issues are shown on a list. Each issue can then be quickly assessed for its urgency and importance. This list also helps to organize and assess decision making for the sub-tasks as well.

| Issues | Current urgent | Future important |
| --- | --- | --- |
| Office refurbishment | no | no |
| Vacation schedules | yes | no |
| Staff allocation | yes | yes |
| Insurance benefits | no | yes |

In the list illustrated here, the manager believes that office refurbishment is neither urgent nor important in the long term. Although there is money budgeted for this project and much discussion about colors and materials has occurred, the proposal originated at the company's headquarters 300 miles away. Staff are enthusiastic but are also happy with their office as it is. This is also the department's busiest season and they are all feeling highly pressured by their work requirements.

The next item, vacation schedules, is an urgent matter for the short term because staff need to make vacation plans with their families. Even so, the actual schedule of dates does not have long-term significance for the department. As long as everyone receives their fair amount of vacation time and their family needs are given consideration, the staff are usually well satisfied.

However, staff allocation for new project work is not only urgent but also has long-term importance to the department. Several projects are now almost complete and new assignments must be given in advance to allow initial preparation to occur. This decision is also extremely important because skillful scheduling has a direct impact on departmental productivity and the overall budget.

The decision about the insurance benefits package is not due for several weeks. Although the staff have received the background information on the available options, it is unlikely that they have all read it thoroughly as yet. This is necessary because the final decision will lock the department into a single package of health care for an indefinite period. This isn't a decision to be taken lightly or quickly. It is enough at this stage to remind staff that the deadline for a decision is in another month.

After examining the list of issues, it becomes obvious that attention should be given first to the work allocation issue because this decision is both urgent and important. Because vacation schedules are also urgent, these should be addressed immediately as well. In fact, all of the information gathered for the new work schedules also serves the task of organizing vacation leave. These two urgent tasks can readily be completed in coordination.

In contrast, the office refurbishment is a low priority in terms of both urgency and importance and so it should be delayed until the department's work load slows down. Although its enthusiasts are likely to understand this, presentation of the list makes a convincing case for postponement.

*Activity*

◆ Make a list of issues that require you to make a decision.

◆ Which are main issues?

◆ Which items on the list are sub-tasks of a main issue?

◆ Organize the list so that it highlights the main tasks. Sub-tasks should be grouped under each main task.

◆ Notice if any sub-tasks contribute to completion of more than one main issue. Put a star next to these items.

◆ Assess the identified main tasks on a list as done in the example.

## SETTING CLEAR GOALS

Identification of priorities allows leaders to focus on the urgent and important decisions first. The successful outcome of these decisions then depends upon setting the right goals. This can seem an obvious point because the priority itself provides the goal. Unfortunately, goals at the outset of a decision-making process are often too vague and general to give sufficient direction.

To illustrate this challenge, the office refurbishment item from the previous section offers a useful example. The goal "office refurbishment" can be interpreted in a variety of ways. It could mean new paint, carpet, and furniture. Sub-tasks as a result would include choice of color schemes, materials, and layout design. The goal could also mean a complete physical overhaul in order to prepare for future electronic installations.

Clarity about the desired end result for "office refurbishment" guides the generation and eventual assessment of the available options. Clearly stated goals allow a group of decision makers to speak the same language. Much decision-making time is wasted because individuals lack a shared understanding of what specifically is required of their decision. Options are therefore proposed, discussed, selected, or rejected in an almost random fashion as decision makers speak at cross-purposes.

Alternatively, when a desired end result is clearly stated and understood, decision makers can more easily generate options. Agreement about the decision's goals makes choosing a course of action considerably easier. A goal gives decision makers a standard against which they can measure their options. The choice that best serves their goal is the one that is most appropriate.

> *A goal is a general and realistic aim for achievement. In decision making, it makes explicit the requirements and the desired end result for the decision.*

Goals give direction to the decision-making process. Even so, the need to achieve a specific outcome must also be balanced with a flexible attitude. On occasion, overly high expectations inhibit success because the criteria for selecting an option are too rigid.

## Defining goals

The following are examples of business issues requiring decisions.

◆ to raise the company's profile in the community

◆ to reduce customer complaints by 10 percent

◆ to purchase a two-acre piece of land adjoining the company's current headquarters

These goals are organized in order of the amount of detail they include. The way each goal is stated illustrates a different stage of the decision-making process.

The first goal is the most general. It is a useful approach at the beginning of the decision-making process. It states in general terms a desired end result so that participants can generate a variety of options. These options can then be examined individually.

As a discussion continues, the decision makers become clearer about what they need to achieve and so they are able to narrow the focus of their debate. For example, options that could be generated to raise the company's profile might include

◆ sponsoring a marathon.

◆ getting press coverage for community service projects.

◆ a director joining the local school board.

As these options are discussed, decision makers discover their varying interpretations of "profile in the community." This allows them to clarify the purpose that they intend their decision to serve.

The second goal is more specific because it includes an exact measurement for the decrease in complaints. Any option that fails to meet this criterion could then be readily eliminated. When a specific quantity or precise detail is included in a decision-making goal, there should be a strong reason. Details enhance the goal *only if* they are valid and necessary. Otherwise, good options that do not provide the exact outcome must be eliminated.

The third goal is very specific. It limits decision making to those options that meet its several precise criteria. This kind of goal serves decision makers who have already determined *what* they need to do. Their next step is to decide *how* to do it.

### State intentions

Goal setting is an important step in the decision-making process. It can be used to generate new options or to narrow the focus and eliminate less appropriate options. When formulating goals, decision makers should make explicit what they want to achieve through their discussion of goals. The more important the decision, the more time is required for this process. Even so, misunderstanding is avoided when participants recognize that goal setting serves different purposes at different stages of the decision-making process.

## A SYSTEMATIC APPROACH

There are always risks involved in decision making. The most obvious is making the wrong decision. Hidden forces and unforeseen circumstances can undermine the best decisions. A careful study of all available information leads to more effective decisions.

### Testing the options

One method for rational decision making begins with a thorough analysis of all of the available options. This process reveals the relative merits of each proposed course of action. Having defined a goal—that is, the desired end result of the decision—the next step is to distinguish the primary requirements from any secondary requirements. This provides a means for weighing the merits of each choice.

Making a decision about a vacation destination offers a useful illustration of this process. There are often real constraints in terms of timing, costs, and method of travel that provide examples of primary requirements. Certain criteria are so important that failure to meet them means cancellation of the vacation. For example, the following three features are the *primary requirements* for two individuals who decide to vacation together.

*Primary*

◆ seven days available

◆ $800 maximum budget

◆ warm and sunny climate

In addition to these primary features, they also have some secondary requirements associated with their decision. Although these criteria are important to them as well, they are not as critical as the primary requirements. Their secondary requirements are as follows.

*Secondary*

◆ resort on the beach

◆ travel and hotel package

◆ popular location

◆ active social and night life

◆ comfortable transportation

◆ stable exchange rate

◆ native language widely spoken

Another list helps to organize all of the available information.

| **Desired end result:** to take a fun vacation away from home | | | |
|---|---|---|---|
| **Primary requirements** | **A**<br>**La Riviera**<br>**Plage** | **B**<br>**Club**<br>**Bahama** | **C**<br>**Mazatlan**<br>**Mar** |
| **1** seven days available | 1 day's travel | 1 day's travel | 1 day's travel |
| **2** $800 maximum | $1,200 | $650 | $600 |
| **3** warm and sunny climate | – | yes | yes |

The desired end result is to have a fun vacation away from home. This makes explicit that the vacation should provide relaxation as well as a break from routine. Therefore, destinations that offer educational opportunities or job-related contacts are not options. Clarity at this initial stage about the decision-makers' intentions reduces any confusion later.

In this example, there are three possible destinations, all of which have been highly recommended to the two decision makers. Each of these is shown on the list across the top row in spaces A to C. The primary requirements are listed down the column on the left side of the page.

Next, each of the destinations should be examined against the primary requirements. As soon as an option fails, it is disqualified. Occasionally, decision makers reveal that they have an attachment to one of the options by saying, "Well, perhaps I can be flexible about that feature after all." This means that it *was not* a primary requirement and should be added to the list of secondary requirements instead. *Primary* is exactly that: if the option does not meet this feature then it fails the decision's requirements.

Option A is La Riviera Plage. Travel from their home requires an entire day each way. This would still allow five days in the resort and so this option just barely passes. Even so, the vacation costs

$1,200 as a minimum figure and so it is too expensive. Although the decision makers hesitate a bit, they realize that this feature effectively disqualifies this option.

Option B is Club Bahama. Travel is half a day each way. It costs less than $800 and the climate there is always sunny and warm. Because it meets all three criteria, it remains an option. This is also true of Mazatlan Mar. This process leaves two options for final consideration. Now the secondary requirements must be considered.

| Secondary requirements | B | C |
|---|---|---|
| 1  resort on the beach | 10 | 8 |
| 2  travel and hotel package | 7 | 7 |
| 3  popular location | 9 | 9 |
| 4  active social and night life | 9 | 9 |
| 5  comfortable transportation | 10 | 7 |
| 6  stable exchange rate | 9 | 5 |
| 7  native language widely spoken | 7 | 9 |
| *Total* | 61 | 54 |

When the decision makers first made this list of secondary requirements, they thoroughly discussed what was most important to them about the vacation. This makes it easier for them to complete the rest of the list. They now give a score to each of their options in terms of how well they match the secondary requirements.

Each option has a maximum score of ten points to be scored against each of the seven listed features. If the option matches the requirement exactly, then it should receive all ten points. For example, option B is located on a clean and sandy beach. Therefore it gets all ten points. Option C is located along the side of a harbor and is a five-minute walk away from the beach. Although it is ocean side, it gets only eight points because it doesn't entirely match the requirement.

The decision makers proceed to score the options against each of the other six features, estimating how closely each matches the requirement. When this process is completed, they total the scores. In this case, option B is clearly the winner. Also, the decision makers have had a chance to discuss their vacation priorities thoroughly through scoring each feature together. When the final decision is made to go to Club Bahama, they both feel that they took an active part in the process.

## Applications

This method is particularly useful when there is controversy over the available options. A leader in this case would first guide the discussion towards discovering what the primary and secondary requirements are. This gives a structure to the debate and allows those who are involved in the decision to express their views easily.

For many decisions, the secondary features each have a different weight, that is, some features are more important for the decision's successful outcome than others. When this is the case, an additional step should be added to the list. Each *feature* should be assigned a weight from one to ten. This shows each feature's *importance*.

As before, each option should also be given a score from one to ten to show the degree to which it matches each of the feature's requirements. This time, though, this score should be multiplied by each feature's weight of importance. When the importance of a feature is included, an option's overall score can be changed dramatically.

For example, the importance score for the sixth requirement on the list could be set at nine because it controls their available spending money. Option B is located in a country with a stable exchange rate and so it receives a score of nine. When this is multiplied by the importance score of nine, this equals 81 points. Option C is located in a country with an unstable rate of exchange and so it receives only five points. When this is also multiplied by nine, it becomes 45 points.

Alternatively, if the feature's importance has only a weight of two, then option B has 18 points (a score of nine multiplied by an importance of two), and C has 10 points (a score of five multiplied by an importance of two). The benefit of including importance in the scoring is revealed when a comparison is made of the feature's scores. If the feature has an importance of nine, the option shows a score of 81 points versus 45 points for that feature. An importance of two shows scores of 18 versus 10.

*Checklist*

◆ Think of one occasion during the day when you made a decision.

◆ Describe this in one or two sentences.

◆ Did you have a clear sense of the decision's priority?

◆ If so, how did you determine this?

◆ How readily did you distinguish between urgency and long-term importance?

◆ Did you have a thorough understanding of the purpose your decision should serve?

◆ If not, how could you improve that understanding?

# Chapter 6

## Creating a Vision

◆

Vision is the distant light that gives direction to any effort. When this is clear and bright, it attracts attention and stimulates curiosity and interest. Even when the details are vague or indistinct, they serve as a reminder that there is more to life than the routine and ordinary. Leaders who offer vision to their colleagues inspire at least as much determined action as those who promise money, status, and influence.

When leaders express vision in a way that touches their supporters, they invite strong commitment. Vision provides the common purpose that leads to united action. Creating a vision is the sixth step to successful leadership development and it is a crucial one. To help you better understand vision, this chapter explores these related topics:

◆ vision and purpose

◆ the big picture

◆ framing and reframing

## VISION AND PURPOSE

In general, visionaries are not the most comfortable kind of people to be around. Particularly if their ideas differ dramatically from conventional views, they are judged by the world to be weirdo, fanatics, or freaks. The determined visionary occasionally contributes to this negative reaction by behaving in an unusual manner.

Even so, it is vision, not the behavior of the visionary, that transforms an ordinary manager or administrator into a leader. Vision empowers individuals and gives them confidence that is both convincing and inspiring to their colleagues. Let us return to the definition of leadership presented in the first chapter of this book:

*Leadership is the ability to present a vision so that others want to achieve it. It requires skill in building relationships with other people and organizing resources effectively. Mastery of leadership is open to everyone.*

Managers and administrators simply present ideas, proposals, memos, and suggestions. They can demand, insist, direct, convince, and encourage their colleagues to cooperate. Depending upon their degree of power and influence, they can also be successful. However, while effective management deserves both praise and reward, it is not leadership.

Leaders have vision, take risks, present dreams, explore possibilities and in general invite their colleagues to join them for a journey into the unknown. Managers read reports, analyze data, and ask their colleagues to meet them in the conference room after lunch. Even when leaders blend perfectly into their organizational surroundings, there is something just a little bit different about them. On close examination, that something is often vision.

*Activity*

◆ Close your eyes and reflect on how well you actually achieve your full potential—personally as well as professionally.

◆ What new feature, behavior, or activity would enhance your life—personally as well as professionally?

◆ What would symbolize this addition in terms of a single word, an object, or an image?

◆ What would you like your future to be like—personally as well as professionally?

◆ Is there any image or situation that summarizes this dream?

This activity begins the process of developing a personal sense of vision. Whenever individuals lift their attention from routine matters, they open themselves up to new possibilities. The ability to envision, to imagine something new and better, to dream, can be acquired with practice. The necessary effort is worthwhile because vision is an essential ingredient for leadership.

Even so, the decision to be a leader rather than a perfectly adequate boss or manager should not be taken lightly. The front line is far more dangerous than the back. Both the demands and the challenges of leadership are far greater than those of routine administration. It has already been suggested that the presenters of vision are not always comfortable people. They also are not always popular.

Leadership requires a high degree of personal commitment and the loss of much personal choice. The glamor of presenting a vision doesn't soften the blow if it is rejected or is widely misunderstood. This experience is far more painful for a leader than is refusal of a proposal, idea, or working paper for a manager. Leaders by definition have the kind of relationship with their supporters that makes them more vulnerable to their reactions. However tough some leaders may appear, is it *really* possible for anyone to avoid feeling hurt when their most deeply felt ideas are rejected?

Leaders who are aware of this danger create stability for themselves through feeling confident that they are *truly* the right choice for their position. They achieve this because they know it is their unique blend of personal qualities that calls them to serve their group at this time. Their sense of vision has guided them to consider carefully the purpose they serve through leadership. Although vision creates vulnerability, it also provides an immense source of strength.

## THE BIG PICTURE

Courage in the face of adversity frequently stems from knowing that the difficulties will eventually end. Like the hero in an action film, a leader needs to believe in the possibility of a positive outcome for each conflict, crisis, or challenge. Leaders more than anyone else are in charge of promoting a belief in a happy ending, even if this seems only the remotest possibility.

"Big picture thinking" allows them to achieve this with credibility. This refers to the ability to shift attention from the details of an immediate situation to see how these fit into the big picture.

In this way leaders gain fresh perspective and often find solutions to nagging problems. Just as each individual fits into a larger family group, separate events occur in relationship to one another. Thinking in terms of the big picture focuses on these relationships so that a new image appears.

For example, a request to a department to cut its expenses could be viewed as part of a bigger picture of the company's finances. This could show that the company is facing a loss if its costs are not reduced. The decision to ask a department to cut expenses could be the result of a wish to avoid duplicated costs.

The big picture highlights the possibility of a positive outcome in this case. On occasion, big picture thinking can reveal hidden threats or potential weaknesses. Leaders are then able to take action before difficulties arise.

The big picture offers a view of a company or group as a whole. Artificial divisions fall away when people and events appear in a larger context. Sometimes this is called "helicopter viewing"—that is, going up mentally to examine the whole of an area of activity. This perspective emphasizes patterns of behavior and draws attention to anything that doesn't fit.

*Activity*

1. Focus attention on one observed interaction between two or three people.

**2.** How would you describe the interaction in terms of:

♦ the purpose for the contact?

♦ the gain or loss for each person as a result of the contact?

♦ any underlying emotions, positive or negative?

♦ any expressed emotion, positive or negative?

♦ achievements from the exchange?

**3.** Now, imagine that there is a cable connecting each person in this exchange. Mentally follow each of these cables to trace all of the activity that led to the observed interaction.

**4.** These activities contribute to the big picture for this interaction.

**5.** Once you develop this big picture, reconsider the list of questions in item 2.

## FRAMING AND REFRAMING

In the dictionary, framing is defined as "an established order or system, or the way that a thing may be constructed, organized, or formed." It is also a term used to describe the *habits of mind* that people develop to view and interpret the world. This topic is touched upon in the Chapter 4 section on bias, because rigid frames of reference contribute to the creation of biased thinking.

Each person frames the world in a unique way, so that two people who witness the same events may interpret them differently. Frames are based on personal values, background, and understanding. Like other habits, frames can be changed; this, though, takes effort and commitment. Big picture thinking is an example of challenging a frame of reference.

Shifting perspective in this way is healthy, creative, and leads to innovative ideas. The process of mentally stepping back, up, or away from a frame is called reframing. This refers to making a conscious choice to interpret the world in a new way. The first step is to identify the frame given to a situation. This usually consists of the story or interpretation that an individual gives to events.

The facts of an exchange are often indisputable. The frames given to an exchange are often as different as the number of people who observe it. For example, every Friday, three colleagues meet at the coffee machine and talk about their weekend plans. The boss observes this and frames the exchange as: these three are always wasting time. The office outcast frames the observed meeting as: those three are always together and are such close friends. The office organizer frames them as: an opportunity to embarrass all three together into contributing to the local charity fund drive.

Based on their different priorities and frames of reference, each person interprets what they see and hear in a manner unique to them.

The point is for leaders to recognize this about themselves and accept that theirs is just one of many possible interpretations. Those who are unwilling to see this limit themselves and their leadership ability.

Although lenders can be praised for single-mindedness, this is a short step away from rigid thinking. Their challenge is to slow down the process of interpreting events until all of the facts are known and then to question whether there are any reframes possible for what is seen and heard.

*Activity*

◆ Choose a new magazine or journal. Look through this until a picture attracts your attention.

◆ Without reading any explanation for the picture, interpret what you see.

◆ This is your frame.

◆ Now, look at the picture again. Challenge yourself to tell a completely different story about the events and people in this picture.

◆ Imagine:
  – different emotions being expressed
  – different motives and intentions
  – different power relationships

◆ This is your reframe.

The skill of reframing is a valuable one for leaders. It encourages development of insight as well as mental flexibility. It applies to creating vision. When individuals are locked into interpreting what they see and hear as a single frame, they lack the capacity to envision. Reframing creates the possibility of new outcomes and new ideas. Leaders need the zest that a truly open mind allows them to experience.

*Checklist*

◆ Think of an event during the day that was important to you.

◆ How did you interpret what occurred?

◆ Is this the usual way for you to interpret events?

◆ If so, can you summarize your mental habits when this kind of event occurs?

◆ Did you make an effort to discover other possible interpretations of what occurred?

◆ If not, reframe the event now.

◆ Consider one, if there is at least one, positive outcome as a result of reframing this event.

◆ What is the big picture for this event?

# Chapter 7

## Taking Charge

♦

The seventh step to successful leadership draws upon the skills, knowledge, and experience gained through this book. Each step highlights an important leadership topic. These include personal development and awareness, relationships with colleagues and understanding motivation, the right use of power, communication skills, decision making, and the creation of vision.

Improved performance means that leaders must take charge of their thinking about each of these topics as well as take charge of changing their behavior. This chapter's activities review the book. The review assesses the strengths and weaknesses of leadership performance in terms of the six topics in this book. The book activities identify what went well and what went badly. This provides information to create a plan of action for further leadership development.

## CHAPTER 1 REVIEW: DEVELOPING AWARENESS

There is great value for individuals in knowing their limitations. Once leaders know their limitations they can learn how to stretch their ability with new skills, knowledge, and experience.

◆ Consider your overall performance as a leader during the past week.

◆ It helps to focus on how you began work each day.

◆ What qualities did you express consistently throughout the week?

◆ What attention did you give to creating positive relationships with your colleagues?

◆ List three strengths in the way you made contact with your colleagues.

◆ How can you build upon these strengths?

◆ List three weaknesses in your behavior towards your colleagues.

◆ What quality or qualities do you need to develop in order to improve upon these weaknesses?

## CHAPTER 2 REVIEW: UNDERSTANDING PEOPLE

Successful leaders know how to speak directly to people's needs, hopes, and dreams. Recognizing and respecting these needs creates bonds of loyalty and trust between leaders and their supporters.

◆ Consider how able you were to identify with your colleagues during the past week.

◆ It helps to focus on their reactions to you when you asked them to do something for you.

◆ Do any of your colleagues merge as part of an indistinct group?

◆ How can you learn more about each person so that their individual strengths and weaknesses become clear?

◆ List three strengths about the way you go about understanding other people.

◆ How can you build upon these strengths?

◆ List three weaknesses about the way you go about understanding other people.

◆ What pattern of behavior do you need to change in order to improve upon these weaknesses?

## CHAPTER 3 REVIEW: POWER AND AUTHORITY

Leaders have power, authority, and responsibility. They need to exercise these and also empower their colleagues to take initiative and responsibility as well. It requires confidence for leaders to invite challenge, questions, and comments from their colleagues. It is also a sign of strong leadership.

◆ Consider the way in which you exercised power during the week.

◆ It helps to remember those activities for which you have responsibility.

◆ Were you able to distinguish the kind of power needed for each situation?

◆ List three strengths about the way you exercised power or took responsibility.

◆ How can you build upon these strengths?

◆ List three weaknesses in your style of leadership.

◆ What do you need to do in order to feel safe about trying a different style?

## CHAPTER 4 REVIEW: COMMUNICATION

Communication skills benefit all areas of a person's life, not only leadership development. Too often the ability to communicate is taken for granted when in fact it is very difficult. Even casual information exchange creates the potential for complete misunderstanding.

◆ Consider your overall communication performance during the week.

◆ It helps to focus on exchanges with people you don't know very well. These rely more on skill than personal familiarity for successful information exchange.

◆ What areas of social skill need further attention and what steps can you take to develop these social skills?

◆ List three strengths for your ability to listen and three strengths for your ability to present information through speaking.

◆ How can you build upon all of these strengths?

◆ List three weaknesses for your listening skills and three weaknesses for your ability to present information through speaking.

◆ How can you transform these and improve your performance?

## CHAPTER 5 REVIEW: DECISION MAKING

Decisiveness is an essential quality for leadership and decision-making skills are required for effective performance. It takes discrimination and judgment to prioritize information and set goals in preparation for making decisions.

◆ Consider your decision-making activity during the week.

◆ It helps to focus on a decision that caused you some stress.

◆ Did you use a systematic approach—that is, did you consider information or priorities in a rational way and set clear goals?

◆ Did any decision just get made because circumstances took over and made the decision for you?

◆ List three strengths in the way that you make decisions.

◆ How can you build upon these strengths?

◆ List three weaknesses in the way that you make decisions.

◆ What actions can you take to improve upon these weaknesses?

## CHAPTER 6 REVIEW: CREATING A VISION

This development area is most difficult to master and yet yields the greatest reward. The ability to imagine new possibilities and create new solutions is highly valued. It is suggested that with determined practice, anyone can learn to work creatively with vision.

◆ Consider your performance as a manager or administrator during the week.

◆ How frequently did you elicit new ideas or comments from your colleagues?

◆ Did you focus all of your management time on solving current problems and dealing with routine business?

◆ How can you give yourself more time to create vision in both your personal and professional life?

◆ How can you work to achieve more of your potential?

◆ List three strengths for the way you are able to see the larger context for a single activity.

◆ How can you build upon these?

◆ List three weaknesses for the way in which you review new solutions and ideas.

◆ How can you challenge yourself to be more creative?

# INDEX

Advocates, 3, 59
Ambition, 9
Ambitious and assertive, 22–26
Analytic and cautious, 22–26
Anarchy, 53
Applications, 71
Appreciation:
   mutual, 4, 53
Approach:
   systematic, 58, 67, 92
Attitude:
   defensive, 5
   flexible, 64
   towards audience, 45
Authority, 29, 34, 38
   emerged from supporters, 26
   exercising, 32
   leaders have, 90
Awareness, 9, 88

Behavior, 4, 13, 19, 30
   actual, 6
   autocratic leader's, 37
   changing, 9, 12, 22, 88
   coherent, 50
   communication, 52
   complex, 43
   controlled, 51
   conventional leadership, 25
   improving, 12
   leadership, 5
   negative, 10, 11, 12
   new, 79
   patterns of, 21, 22, 24, 81, 90
   positive, 10, 12
   specific, 12
   towards colleagues, 89
   visionary, 77
   weaknesses in, 2, 89, 90
Benefits:
   autocratic, 35

democratic, 35
permissive, 35
Bias, 43–45, 82
Biased thinking, creation of, 82
Big picture, 80–82, 85
Blanchard, Ken, 36

Caring and supportive, 22, 23, 26
Charisma, 3
Coaching, 53, 56
Coherent, 50–52, 56
Colleagues, 6, 19, 22, 29–33,
      38–42, 90
   behavior towards, 89
   comments, 5
   feedback from, 29
   ideas, 53
   leader criticizes, 51
   limitations of, 21
   motivation, 26
   negative beliefs, 8
   opinions and beliefs, 8
   perceptions, 9
   point of view, 10, 29
   positive beliefs, 8
   strengths, 20
   underdeveloped, 34
   weaknesses, 20
Commitment, 82
   lack of, 16
   personal, 79
   receipt of, 26
   strong, 76
Common purpose, 4
Communication, 42–44, 48,
      49–56, 88
   goal-directed, 50
   performance, 91
   skills, 91
Competition, 42
Comprehension, 21

Concentration, 23
Confidence, 17, 29, 34, 77, 90
    act with, 58
    appearance of complete, 16
    vision gives, 77
Conflict, 80
Confusion, 53, 59, 68
Contribution:
    creative, 53
Controversy, 55, 71
Courage, 10, 80
Creating understanding, 43
Creativity, 18, 19
Crisis:
    positive outcome for, 80
Curiosity, 29
Cynicism, 21

Decision:
    best, 67
    circumstances made the, 92
    deadline for, 62
    final, 62, 71
    priority, 73
    successful outcome of, 71
    wrong, 67
Decision making, 58, 69–71, 88,
    92
    activity, 92
    process
        different stage of, 65
        outset of, 63
    rational, 67
    skills, 92
    time wasted in, 64
Decisiveness, 92
Delegation, 28, 37, 38, 40
Democracy, 34
Democratic:
    benefits, 35
    frustrations, 35
Determination, 16, 17
Development:
    of awareness, 89

    of self-awareness, 2
    personal, 2, 11, 88
Dictator, 34
Digression, 55
Discrimination, 92
Disloyalty, 16
Dissent, 53
Dreams, 78, 89

Electronic:
    means, 51
    systems, 31, 32
    technology, 31
Emotions, 17, 42
    different, 84
    positive, 82
    negative, 82
Empowerment, 38
Experience, 13, 30, 31, 43
    gained, 88
    new, 89
Expertise, 31

Fairness, 54
Fear, 17
Feedback, 5, 28, 29
    negative, 11, 12
    positive, 12
Feelings, 42
Frame of reference, 82, 83
Framing, 82, 83
Frustrations, 54, 55
    autocratic, 35
    democratic, 35
    permissive, 35

Gestures, 44–46
Goals:
    clear, 58, 63, 64
    decision-making, 64, 66
    decision's, 64
    defining, 64, 67
    discussion of, 66
    for development, 13

formulating, 66
give direction to, 64
performance, 5, 39
personal, 52, 56
professional, 52, 56
setting, 66, 92
specific, 65
Growth, 17

*Habits of mind*, 82
Helicopter viewing, 81
Hersey, Paul, 36
Hidden messages, 45
Hierarchy of needs, 18, 20
Humility, 11
Humor, 12

Identifying priorities, 58
Impatience, 21
Importance:
    feature's, 71
    long-term, 73
    score, 72
Influence, 76, 78
Innovative ideas, 83
Inspiration, 16, 25
Integrity, 7, 30
Intelligence, 42
Interdependence, 36, 58
Intervention, 53–56

Job satisfaction, 20
Job security, 21
Judgment, 10, 34, 44, 92

Knowledge, 13, 88
    new, 89

Leaders:
    best, 3
    born, 2
    following the, 2
    performance of, 89
    potential, 4

qualities of, 3, 9, 10
tasks, 4
Leadership:
    autocratic, 37
    basics, 2
    democratic, 33
    designated, 31
    develop essentials for, 4
    development of, 13
    effective, 20
    effectiveness of, 5
    experience of, 6, 7
    improved performance of, 6
    isolated, 32
    mastery of, 4
    nature of, 3
    negative behavior of, 6–10
    performance
        strengths, 88
        weaknesses, 88
    permissive, 33, 34
    positive behavior of, 6, 7, 9
    potential of, 4
    power of, 30
    practice, 7, 20
    qualities of, 17
    responsibility, 28
    skills, 5, 6
    solutions, 21
    strong, 29, 90
    style, 28, 37, 40
        autocratic, 33, 34
        existing, 9
        fair, 54
        weaknesses in, 91
    successful, 14, 16
    technique, 39
    topic, 88
List:
    decision making, 61
    primary requirements, 68
    secondary requirements, 70
Listening and speaking, 43
Loyalty, 3, 26, 53

bonds of, 89
group, 53

Managing power, 28
Maslow, Abraham, 36
Motivation, 16–22, 39, 42
  understanding, 88
Motives:
  different, 84
  negative, 17
  positive, 17
Mystique, 25

Opinion free-for-all, 53
Options:
  available, 67
  good, 66
  testing, 67

Paraphrasing, 53–56
Personal achievement, 19
Personal development, 5, 9
Personality, unique, 9
Personal quality, 10
Perspective, 81
  shifting, 83
Positive force, 23
Positive outcome, 80, 81, 85
Power, 26, 28, 30, 40
  alternative kinds of, 39
  and authority, 28
  charismatic, 30, 31
  degree of, 78
  designated, 30
  exercised, 90
  expert, 30, 31
  information, 30, 31
  leaders have, 90
  managing, 28
  mistaken use of, 32
  mongering, 39
  needed, 90
  relationships, 84
  right use of, 88

source of, 32
  through bullying, 4
  through manipulation, 4
Principles, 20
Priorities, 58–60, 63, 71, 92
  decision's, 73
  different, 83
  group's, 22
Pyramid, 18

Recognition, 4, 20
Reframing, 82–85
Relationship:
  building, 4, 78
  colleagues, 88
  family, 19
  group, 36
  interdependent, 26
  positive, 3, 25, 28, 89
  power, 84
  strong, 25
  team, 19
Requirements:
  primary, 67, 69, 71
  secondary, 67–71
Respect, 3, 4, 21, 25, 53, 54
Responsibility:
  leaders have, 90
  sharing, 36
  took, 90
Rewards, 16, 21, 23, 78
Risk-taking, 42

Self-acceptance, 11
Self-assessment, 5, 8
Self-awareness, 2, 7, 22
Self-confidence, 10, 18
Self-control, 51, 52, 56
Self-discipline, 51
Self-doubt, 16
Self-esteem, 19
Self-image, 5, 10
Self-questioning, 16
Sensitivity, 19

Skills, 13, 35, 88, 91
  acquiring, 59
  communication, 26, 42, 50,
    52, 91
  decision-making, 58
  discussion, 53
  new, 89
  personal, 30
  reframing, 84
  social, 43, 49, 52, 91
    controlled, 51
Solitude, 23
Solutions:
  creating new, 92
  review new, 93
Speaker:
  credilibity of, 50
  gestures of, 52
  movement of, 52
  voice of, 52
Speaking, 47, 91
  techniques include
    headlining, 47–49
    pacing, 47–49
    summarizing, 47–49
Specific outcome, 64
State intentions, 66
Survival, 17, 19, 21

Talent, 30, 35
Teamwork, 21
Tolerance, 29
Trust, 10, 89

Understanding, 44, 82
  creating, 52
  improve, 73
  people, 89

Values, 16, 20, 21
  personal, 82
Vision, 4, 20, 21, 76–92
  creating a, 92, 93
  work creatively with, 92
Visionaries, 77
Visual signals, 43–46
Vocal sounds, 43–46
Vulnerability, 80

Weakness, 17, 33, 88–93
Weight, 72
  different, 71
Work satisfaction, 21